HUES OF THE HEART

A COLLECTION OF POEMS ABOUT HOPE, DESPAIR, AND MATTERS OF THE HEART

ALTHEA R. GONSALVES

Made with ♥ on the Notion Press Platform
www.notionpress.com

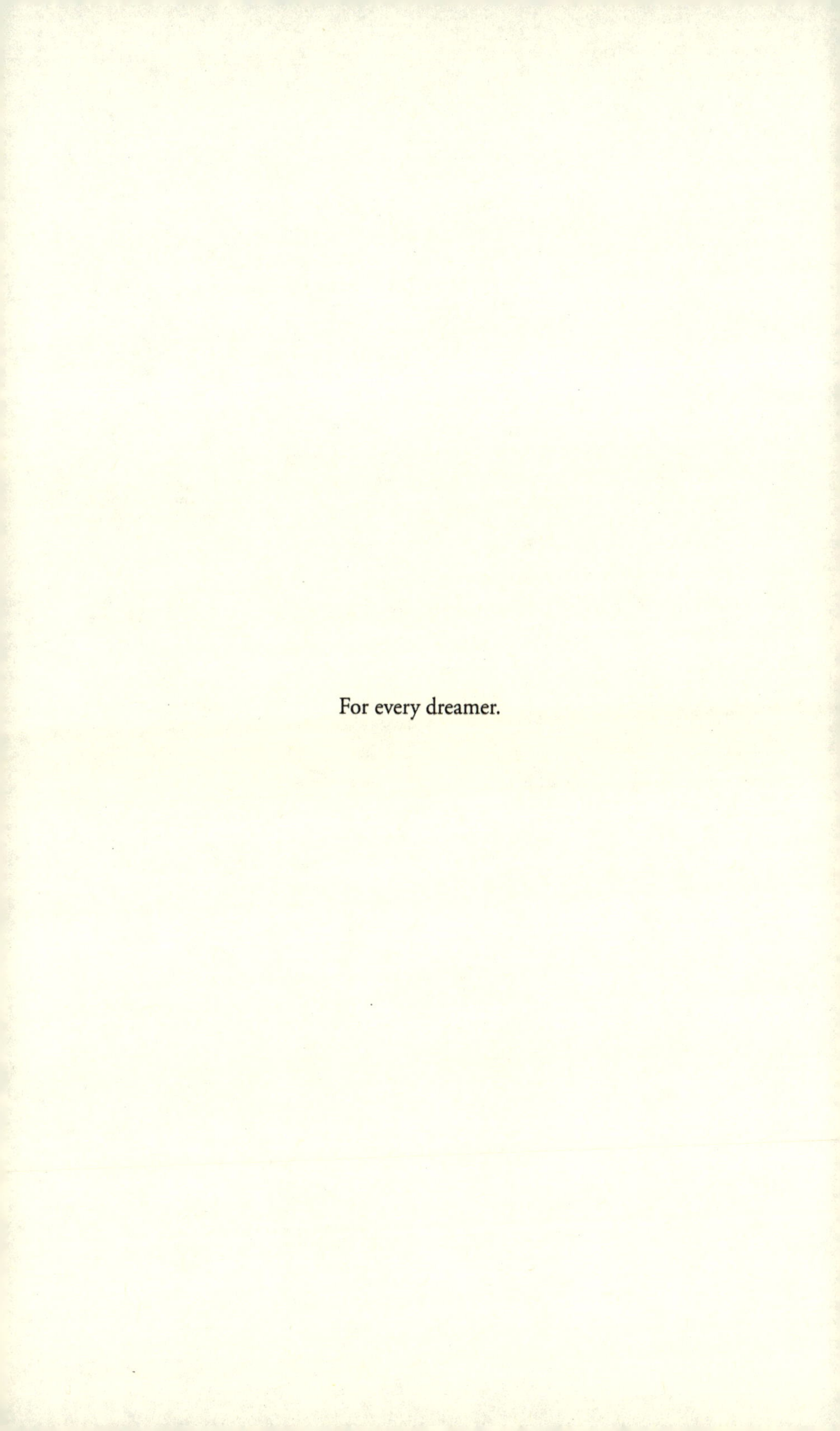

For every dreamer.

Contents

Contents

Acknowledgements

I would like to thank Notion Press for the seamless process of publishing this book.

I feel great gratitude for my friends, family, and all my readers, who supported Hues of Hope and encouraged me to keep writing.

1. Believe

If the world is not beautiful and life is not worthwhile
And ten tears don't lead to a singular smile
Why would I waste all my effort and time
To capture it all in rhythm and rhyme?
Would I waste my love and the ink in this pen
On something worthless? Tell me, then
Would I write to you if you already knew?
Why am I repeating these lines to you?
If the night's darkness isn't worth the sunrise
And evidence of existence remains when things die,
Isn't the memory of a laugh full of love
That echoes in an empty room enough?
Would I dawdle and stare at meaningless things,
See your heart but not the meaning it brings?
Would a poet like me waste love on a lie
When truthful am I... Tell me, would I?
Accept every bit of goodness you receive
For a heart full of sorrow deserves to believe.

2. Heart on a sleeve

Tell me, is it foolish or brave
To neither flee nor fight
But to pet the wolf and tame it
Run alongside it at night
To look for love in dark corners
Where lingers no lantern bright
To sit by a destructive fire
And to see its warmth and light?
Tell me, is it unnatural or human
To fervently believe?
To wish to comfort demons
And to share the weight they heave
To express and exist openly
And wear one's heart on one's sleeve,
Even with the possibility
It could leap off the fabric and leave-
Tell me, is it worth it to
Befriend these reckless beings
To bestow a kinder gaze on them
When it's clear that they are bleeding
To offer a shoulder or hand
Even with the possibility
That the heart could be broken
Is it worth it to love freely?
It must be.

3. River

I'm proud of you for being here
Still living, learning, growing
Like a river always flowing
What a sight it is to behold
You're parrying life's blows
With such skill that only shows
That you've been here before
How well you've done with all you know!
Maybe you're a little rusty
And your heart's gone a bit dusty
Maybe you're only a trickle
When you were once a steady flow
But this I know, you've been here before
Running down the hill to the shore
Surely, as I write by the bank
It's you that I have to thank
For you're in what I write and draw
In every mark of perfection, and flaw
Art imitates life, don't you see?
You're the river that meets the sea of poetry.

4. Make art, not war

I can't help but get stuck in the spaces called art
The places where I leave pieces of my heart
Standing still in an alley, staring at the walls
Anything to remind me that in this great world, I am small
Running my hand along the towering bookshelves
As different stories begin to introduce themselves
I can't help but draw the stranger in whose eyes I recognize
A rare beauty, that just must be immortalized
Looking at the solemn, graceful face cast in marble
Frozen in time, perfectly poised like a marvel
I can't help marvel at the breath-taking scene
As I'm lit by the moving light of the cinema screen
Heart rising fast as the song rises faster
Strings crescendoeing, heartstrings being mastered
I can't help but make art at a time when love is rarer
And imbue my words and acts with it as its bearer.

5. Nostalgia

Obsidian nights and streetlights
Stars across the sky
Cold air threading through hair
A pensive, dreaming stare
Singing along to an old song
In many memories, it belongs
Nostalgia-ridden smile hidden
The words come to you, unbidden.

6. A spark in the darkness

This world is a dark place
With shadowed corners and painted faces
I thought I could make you smile so wide
That the paint would crack at each side
Your mask would fall and wither
And your breastplate would lose its shimmer,
Chip and break at my touch
I forget that I hope too much
I tried to light the candles
Of those cloaked in cloaks and mantles
Reached out to the armor's crack
But they stayed in the pitch black
My dream of starting a fire
Burns away on a pyre
But the flame behind my eyes
Never dies though darkness tries
I'm saving it to light your heart up someday, friend.

7. The tree they grew

I‘m the tree that this world grew
Into a ground cracked and broken
With raging fires and waterless soil
Our blooming season’s stolen
We were once young and home to more
The most beautiful anyone’s seen
Now their leaves are browning to the ground
What does it mean if I’m evergreen?
The infected soil is killing them
I can’t save everyone
There’s snow upon my branches
But I'm growing toward the sun
What does it mean if I make it
And then don’t see this land pure?
What would all the suffering mean
That all these stumps had to endure?
There are times when we must shed our leaves
But do not cut us down
Nurture us, the old land’s young trees
Let us replenish the ground
My friends, my lovely forest
I wish you not to freeze and die
Someday the rain will pour
And our hope will scarce run dry.

8. Human

Sometimes I find myself thinking
This maudlin mind is a curse
That reds and whites, all-too-bright lights,
They might be a shade worse
Than grey walls and machine-like things
Monotone, frozen scapes
But with the sunlight streaming in
Why should I draw the drapes?
I am a human after all
With an all too human heart
That melts at fine placement of words
And walls that frame fine art
With access to a grand spectrum
Why should I keep myself out?
Why curse myself for loving the rain
And risk the coming of a drought?
When I'm full with an emptiness
I long for what I cursed
The ocean of emotion
In which I should wish to be immersed.

9. Save

They say you can't save everyone
I know this, well and good
Those tired eyes when day is done
A sigh that means no good
I hear the screams and anguished cries
The steadily fraying rope
I see the desperate, longing tries
The slow decay of hope
The vacant stare of sweet despair
How a thought consumes a mind
I've seen the idea float in the air
The what-if that makes them blind
It captures them in its talons
A vile and monstrous thing
They see a saviour without horns
But pristine, white, beating wings
Getting older is a fearsome thing
And life seems like a curse
How do I hold those hurting
Without making their pain worse?
I promise I only mean well
But don't know how to do good
They save you can't save everyone, well
How I wish I could.

10. Untitled

I learned this the hard way
That poetry is no gold
No sparkling or pure thing
No remedy of old
It's a long line of human beings
Coping and hopelessly hoping
Despairing and deeply caring
Self-destructing and self-repairing
It's startling clarity
And it's lost, hazy confusion
Faces of smiles and tear stains
Mottled with contusions
It's an elegant and broken thing
It's outstanding and so normal
It's a human response to everything
So ethereal and so mortal
Just like each one of us
And if we see it as art
Perhaps we should view ourselves
With the same awe, kindness and presence of heart.

11. Ode to my heart

Oh heart, true heart, you stand so strong
Steadily beating in bars and measures
Of my love's ballad and battlesong
Thou art the greatest of all my treasures
Just as I, you proudly sing
Behind a cage; your notes slip through
Preaching all that's great and good
In a crooked world, an admirable thing
it is that you remain so true
In a world so filled with falsehood.

12. Sink

I don't mean to do it, but I still deeply sink
Into everything I love, and everything I think
Always leading with my heart and barely heeding my head
Weaving poems for the lovely morning before I make the bed
I don't mean to do it but I seep onto the page
I travel through the books and films, I live in every age
I learn new languages, I immerse myself in songs
I dream in far-off lands and come home, where my heart belongs
I sink into the poem, into the work, into the sight
Into the starry sky and the rainy mid-July
Into a silent dream of the moon in early June
I sink into the present and I surface with a tune
If I'm looking out a window, I will sink into daydreams
I don't mean to do it, but I fall deeply, it seems
I am a poet in everything I do, much less write
Sinking into darkness and coming up with the light.

13. Sail

Take a deep breath
Inhale... and exhale
Close your tired eyes
Ground yourself on today
Are you prouder of yourself
As you're making it through?
Are you thinking of tomorrow
And all the things you have to do?
No, imagine you're sailing
On a sea of white clouds
And the late, twilight sun
Peeks at you, looking proud
Imagine the moon
Watching you in quiet pride
Through its phases and eclipses
Even with its dark side...
Well,
If the moon has its sides
And the sun sets and rises
Why can't your progress look like hills
And valleys of different sizes
Ask yourself what's the next step
Look at the compass, unfurl your sails
Turn your weary sighs
Into full inhales and slow exhales

You can do this, I know it
You've been here before
And even if you haven't,
There's still time to explore
Set sail, unfold your map
Venture into the night
But don't forget to take a breath
And look at the stars, your guiding lights.

14. Oh, love.

A heart carved into woody bark,
Spray-painted on a wall
A note trapped in a locket
With a sweet, besotted scrawl
A love lock on the city bridge
A matching set of rings
Two voices lined in harmony
Oh, hear love as it sings
"I miss you dearly" "As do I"
"How was your day today?"
"Just text me when you get home"
"...You sure you don't want to stay?"
The reassuring smile
A hand on your restless knee
The reflection in the mirror
As you say "I love you, me."

15. Inspiration

Inspiration divine
Fill my inkwell, forsake me not
Give dialogue to my heart
And my mind, a novel thought
I press my waiting ear
Up against the bolted door
Sing me a solemn song,
A sweet sonnet, I implore
Pull my hands' strings
Move the pen across the page
I'm surrounded by several things
I'm a puppet on a stage
Pull on the weary wires
Till they're worn and satisfied
Don't strand me on this strand
Upon the sand, all tongue-tied
Send your blues and rolling waves
Wash me in awe and wonder
Capsize this calm and so bored boat
Into the currents under
Inspiration, fill my mind
Give dialogue to my art
There are still many plays
That do play out in my heart.

16. Labyrinth

In the labyrinth of my mind
The walls are marble-white
Covered in green ivy
Ivory, quartz and calcite
With intricate calligraphy
Engraved on every post
Distant songs from statues' lips
Dwelling like musical ghosts
There are monoliths and obelisks
With names inscribed on them
Tapestries of stories
Ripped apart and torn at the hem
It's all too quiet sometimes
Only ominous rumbles remain
Daydreams dance through the halls
And leave like a rehearsed refrain.
If you're passing through my halls
Write your name on the white, marbled walls.

17. Stars

This chasm of cosmic vastness
I see in every soul
A dotted, light-filled darkness.
A vacancy so whole
That it matches the cosmos
As I stare out into space
As I compose and purge
What I'm composed of with minimal grace
I am mirroring my surroundings
A grain of sand, but I am the shore
My reflections aren't astounding
Or giving the universe more
But I'd like to think my echoes
Though lost in the cosmic vastness
Find hearts, forlorn and morose
And become stars in their darkness.

18. Moment

Gazing out a window
At the dark, never-ending sky
This state of mind is fleeting
And I've always wondered why
This moment of full clarity
Of pensive introspection
Is once a day, mine, and then gone
Evaporating dreams and reflections
This awareness of the moment
Of my presence in the present
Is the joy of being alive
Amid the world's demands incessant
This feel of cold air though my hair
And consciousness of my breaths
The sight of all that's before me
Makes known all the world's depths
All my dreams dance before me
All the answers reveal themselves
The musings of my mind take me
Beyond, to greater realms
They set fire to my sensibility
Burn through all my practical plans
I am only meant to behold the world
To seek and to understand.

19. A pen

All I had was a pen
No scepter and no sword
No tool to make or mend
What must I do? I implored
All I had was a pen
No curled fist or swift feet
No fight, flight or sense godsent
So I wielded it fearfully
In a world of fire and ice
Poisoned like a foe's wine
I had no antidote
Only ink in cursive lines
And though this ink is something
The world can live without,
All I have is this pen
I'll write till it runs out.

20. The writer's dream

I want to sit by a spring
And witness a dawning morning
Singing softly to the wind
Pencil scribbling anything
To write at night with the thunder
My quill would never shudder
Spurred on by cracks of lightning
And the crescent moonshine brightening
I want to create symphonies
Eye-opening epiphanies
Eye-closing lullabies
Of muted colours or butterflies
One day, I want to write something
That can turn something from nothing
Or can make the ground shake
For words can make or break

21. Poetry, poetry

Where people saw rain falling on wet roads
You made me see diamonds falling from the sky
On a glittering, glistening path, in the night
With the glow streaming from the streetlight
And the lights of the city and cars reflect
On the roads, in reds, whites, blues, and yellows
Dark sky of stars, rain, and the moon's glow
Eyes watching tiny rivulets flow
Against the glass- Poetry, what have you done?
My thoughts sound like flowers springing from the ground
Modern language, how it stifles me now
When I'm filled with metaphors wanting to come out
Poetry, poetry, look at this mess
Of colours and lights and ink and designs
That you've injected into my mind
My mind's eye is open where others play blind.

22. Transform

Turn this dirt into a castle
Own the land on which you toil
Wear your crossed heart like a marvel
Plant these seeds into the soil
Use your pain and blood as ink
Bleed your words onto the page
Steer this ship, don't let it sink
Stand at the deck like it's a stage
Turn all your tears into water
Feed the mighty tree inside
Men, they weep and they slaughter
But they'll watch you flower, eyes wide
Turn your thoughts to poetry
Wear your wounds like battle scars
Shed your dead leaves, growing tree
Spread your branches towards the stars.

23. Beware

Beware of what you tell your brain
For it can bring the pouring rain
Even on bright, sunny days, if
You don't care for it more
The mind itself is mind-bending
A house so grand and unending
The smallest, faintest whisper
Could echo forevermore
The sound could stir a tempest there
A cycle of rage and despair
A descent to Erebos' lair
A spiral coiling in
A daily reassurance
That could increase your endurance
Empower you to hold your own,
It must come from deep within
An appreciative echo in your mind
With timbre of a different kind
That kind that you've always known,
The voice inside that is your own,
Will bloom some rarer flowers there
And vines that twine over the stairs
The halls will fill with mellifluous chorus
And set the future's tone.

24. Into the night (emerge with the light)

Go gently into the night
With a lantern glowing bright
Glowing eyes and forest fires
Keep your self in sight
And in the cold and wintry wood
Where many souls once stood
With stronger ropes and weak hope,
Know that you did all you could
Approach with kind and caring eyes
An outstretched hand so wise
No sympathy or pity
No panic or forceful whys
But warm and golden luminescence,
Offer a calming presence
Point at the slow-rising sun
And let be the mindful quiescence
Then venture with the hiding one
With the tear-filled, fear-filled eyes
Guide them into safer lands
Where dark nights mean starry skies
and an impending sunrise.

25. Ever-present star

There's love in your heart even when you think it's empty
There's hope in your hand even when you think there's not
Somewhere out there's a voice calling out for help
Quietly or loudly, lost inside their thoughts
There's a light deep within you that shines when you see
A person who's in need, a feeling of empathy
Shine it like a torch upon those lost in the dark
Not quite like a spotlight, but like an ever-present star
If you're lost in the dark, you're allowed to feel afraid
Feel the fear and rage, but try to be kind anyway
For like you, everyone weathers a storm inside their head
Choose your words carefully, for they cannot be unsaid
Reach out with your hand, ask for help, and give your own
We aren't ever alone, even when we're worn and torn
Love yourself and others and be kind to everyone
Be proud that you are human, that you've made it this far since day one.

26. Paper-thin skin

Paper skin so paper-thin
Drenched and falling apart in the rain
Crumpling from anything
From forceful holds that tear and stain
Their words so carelessly written
But oh, they're felt so deeply though
On paper skin so paper-thin
Denting on the inside just so
Delicate, and strong as well
With the paper's words displayed in bold
It's pain and joy like a show-and-tell:
Here is my story, why is yours untold?
Why won't you let your heart unfold?

27. Not about rain

Windshield wipers glide
Against the rain-lashed window pane
The golden summer turns to grey
And all it does is rain
The sobbing sky's thunderous cries
Its eyes are wet from tears
I sing songs to console it as
I watch the night grow near
When morning comes, the new world is
A green and glistening sight
In bloom, watered by nature's gloom,
The flowers chase the light
From the darkest storms came daisies
From the grey skies came the blue
This poem isn't about rain or the sky, it is about you.

28. The outside

She gave the world her heart
With a smile and open hands
Her head adorned with symphonies
Interwoven with strands
Broken at her doorstep
She had found the glassy shards
Red and jagged at the edges
Marred and scarred and hard
Her dreams ricocheted off
Of the glass encasing her
She pressed her nose against it
And she watched the silence stir
The words in her cracked heart
Found the open air's embrace
They danced around the trees
Pounded 'gainst the glassy case
The cracks are spreading slowly
With each page, book, and word
With each determined will
With every other voice heard
Her lost dreams and symphonies
Watch them as they go
If they ever make it to the outside
I'll be sure to let you know.

29. Heartstrings

The heart has always been the instrument I wish to play
From interest to mastery, I wish to go the way
To hold it till I understand, study until I know
Till I'm gentle like the breeze and like the trees, I bloom and grow
To make tears fall from cold eyes and thaw the season's snow
So when disaster strikes a heart, I'm away by a stone's throw
To slay the blasted tentacles that have you in their hold
So that you'll never have to freeze and shudder in the cold
I wish that when I've mastered the heartstrings like a great bard
I'll know to look upon a landscape, burnt away and marred
And sow the seeds of rebirth, and play broken hearts to life
There's much work to do, but I can get there if I try.

30. Power

To use our hearts to love and care
In a world on fire where warmth is rare
To spread hope where there's endless despair,
That is real power
To choose to see the colours of light,
The spectrum between black and white
To let live every shade of life
That is real power
To try to understand and learn
That hatred makes the whole world burn
And war is a point of no return
That is real power
To think about what we think we know
And challenge it to know even more
To accept that nothing is written in stone
That is real power.

www.ingramcontent.com/pod-product-compliance
Lightning Source LLC
LaVergne TN
LVHW041003150826
845672LV00002B/849

9798891860131